Edition

THE COMPLETE 2024 TOFU COOKBOOK FOR BEGINNERS

A Beginner's Guide to Flavorful Plant-Based Cooking with easy Recipes for Vibrant Health and Culinary Exploration

BONUS

7 Days Meal Planner

VAKARE RIMKUTE

⚠ Disclaimer

The recipes and information in this cookbook are intended for general informational purposes only. While Vakare Rimkute has made every effort to ensure the accuracy and completeness of the content, they make no representations or warranties of any kind, express or implied, about the suitability or applicability of the recipes for any purpose.

INTRODUCTION TO TOFU COOKBOOK FOR BEGINNERS

Welcome to the world of tofu. Whether you're a seasoned vegetarian, a curious omnivore, or just trying to add more variety to your diet, this cookbook will help you discover the wonderful and fascinating world of tofu. Tofu, also known as bean curd, is a common component in many Asian dishes and is gaining popularity globally due to its health advantages and culinary versatility.

This cookbook contains a variety of simple and tasty tofu dishes suitable for beginners. From substantial breakfasts to filling main courses and sumptuous desserts, there's a tofu recipe for each occasion. But before we get into the dishes, let's take time to understand the history and origins of tofu and why it's such a fantastic addition to any diet.

Tofu has a rich history that spans back over 2,000 years. It is said to have originated in China during the Han period **(206 BCE-220 CE)** and then expanded to other countries of Asia, including Japan, Korea, and Southeast Asia. According to legend, tofu was accidentally found when a Chinese chef mixed nigari (a natural coagulant obtained from saltwater) with soy milk, resulting in the development of curds.

Tofu has long been a popular and versatile component of Asian cuisine. It has also gained popularity in Western nations as a healthy and environmentally friendly alternative to meat and dairy products.

So, why should you use tofu in your culinary repertoire? The justification lies in its exceptional versatility and ability to complement various flavours and ingredients. Tofu lends itself to various culinary delights, including savoury stir-fries, luscious desserts, and robust soups.

So, without further ado, let's go on a tofu-filled journey together, where each dish offers a story of flavour, inventiveness, and nutritious deliciousness. Prepare to experience the wonder of tofu and go on a gastronomic journey that will thrill and inspire. Welcome to the beautiful world of tofu—let's get cooking!

TABLE OF Content

TOFU

CHAPTER 1

BASIC OF TOFU

WHAT IS TOFU

Tofu, also known as bean curd, is a popular food derived from soybeans. It is made by curdling fresh soy milk, pressing it into a solid block, and cooling it. Tofu is a staple ingredient in many Asian cuisines and has gained popularity worldwide due to its versatility, nutritional value, and ability to absorb flavours from other ingredients.

Tofu comes in various textures, ranging from soft and silken to firm and extra-firm. The texture is determined by the amount of water pressed during the tofu-making process. Soft tofu is creamy and delicate, while firm tofu holds its shape well and can be grilled, stir-fried, or baked.

DIFFERENT TYPES OF TOFU

1. **Silken Tofu**: Silken tofu has a soft and delicate texture, similar to custard or pudding. It is made by coagulating soy milk without curdling, resulting in a smooth and creamy consistency. Silken tofu is often used in dishes with the desired texture, such as soups, smoothies, desserts, and dressings.

2. **Firm Tofu**: Firm tofu has a higher water content than extra firm tofu, giving it a softer texture while maintaining its shape. It holds together well during cooking and is versatile enough for various dishes. Firm tofu is commonly used in stir-fries, scrambles, salads, and sandwiches.

3. **Extra Firm Tofu**: Extra firm tofu has the lowest water content of the three types, making it dense and sturdy. It holds its shape well, even when subjected to high heat or pressure during cooking. As it retains its texture and does not easily fall apart, extra-firm tofu is ideal for grilling, baking, frying, and stir-frying. It is often used as a meat substitute for tofu steaks, skewers, and stir-fries.

HOW TO STORE TOFU PROPERLY

1. **Keep it Refrigerated:** Tofu is perishable and should always be stored in the refrigerator. Once opened, it needs to be refrigerated immediately.

2. **Store in Water:** If you've bought tofu packed in Water, keep it stored in the Water it came in. This helps to keep the tofu moist and fresh. Change the Water every day or two to prevent it from becoming too sour.

3. **Use an Airtight Container:** If you've removed tofu from its original packaging or water-packed tofu that you've drained, transfer it to an airtight container. Cover the tofu entirely with fresh Water and seal the container tightly before placing it in the refrigerator.

4. **Change the Water Regularly**: If you're storing tofu in Water, change the Water every day or two. This helps to keep the tofu fresh and prevents it from absorbing any off-flavours.

5. **Use Within a Few Days**: Tofu is best when consumed fresh, so try to use it within a few days of purchasing. While tofu can last longer in the refrigerator, its texture and flavour may deteriorate.

6. **Freezing Tofu:** If you don't plan to use tofu within a few days, you can freeze it for later use. To freeze tofu, drain the Water, wrap it in plastic wrap or place it in an airtight container, and store it in the freezer. Frozen tofu can last for several months.

COMMON INGREDIENTS

Tofu	Carrots	Sriracha or chili sauce
Soy sauce	Broccoli	Hoisin sauce
Sesame oil	Mushrooms	Peanut butter or tahini
Vegetable oil	Spinach	Maple syrup or brown sugar
Garlic	Cabbage	Lime or lemon juice
Ginger	Snow peas	Cilantro
Onion	Snap peas	Basil
Scallions	Cornstarch	Red pepper flakes
Bell peppers	Rice vinegar	Tofu marinades
Agave nectar	Nuts and seeds	
Tofu seasonings	Mirin	

WHERE TO FIND TOFU AND SPECIALTY INGREDIENTS

1. **Local Grocery Stores:**
- Many mainstream grocery stores carry tofu in their refrigerated sections. Look for it near other vegetarian or Asian food products.
- Some larger chains may even offer different varieties of tofu, such as silken, firm, or extra-firm.

2. **Asian Markets:**
- Asian grocery stores often have a wide selection of tofu, including fresh tofu made in-house.
- You can also find speciality tofu products like fermented tofu (fermented bean curd) or flavoured tofu.

3. **Health Food Stores:**
- Health food stores and co-ops are great places to find organic and non-GMO tofu options.
- They may also carry speciality products like smoked tofu or tofu-based meat substitutes.

4. **Online Retailers:**
- Many online retailers offer a variety of tofu brands and speciality tofu products.
- This can be a convenient option if you live where tofu is not readily available or are looking for specific types or brands.

5. **Farmers' Markets:**
- Some farmers' markets may have vendors selling homemade or tofu from locally sourced ingredients.
- This is a great way to support local producers and get high-quality tofu.

6. **Specialty Stores:**
- Speciality stores focusing on vegetarian or vegan products may offer a more comprehensive selection of tofu and tofu-based products.
- These stores may also carry speciality ingredients commonly used in tofu recipes, such as nutritional yeast, miso paste, or tamari.

7. **Ethnic Food Aisles:**
- Check the ethnic food aisles in your local grocery store for speciality ingredients commonly used in tofu recipes, such as soy sauce, rice vinegar, sesame oil, and Asian spices.
- In these sections, you may also find tofu-related products like tofu skins or tofu noodles.

Cooking Methods for Tofu

Pan-Frying

- Press the tofu to remove excess water.
- Cut the tofu into desired shapes.
- Heat oil in a pan over medium heat.
- Add tofu pieces and cook until golden brown on each side, flipping occasionally.

Baking

- Preheat the oven to 375°F (190°C).
- Press and slice the tofu into cubes or slabs.
- Marinate the tofu if desired.
- Place tofu on a lined baking sheet and bake for 25-30 minutes, flipping halfway through.

Grilling

- Press and slice the tofu into thick slabs.
- Marinate the tofu for at least 30 minutes.
- Preheat the grill to medium-high heat.
- Grill tofu for 5-7 minutes on each side, or until grill marks form.

Stir-Frying

- Press and cut tofu into cubes or strips.
- Heat oil in a wok or skillet over high heat.
- Add tofu and stir-fry with vegetables and sauces until heated through and slightly crispy.

Boiling

- Cut tofu into cubes or slices.
- Bring a pot of water to a boil.
- Add tofu and let it simmer for 5-10 minutes to heat through.
- Remove tofu from water and pat dry before using in recipes.

Steaming

- Cut tofu into slices or cubes.
- Place tofu in a steamer basket lined with parchment paper or cabbage leaves.
- Steam for 5-10 minutes until heated through.

Cooking Methods for Tofu

Blending

- Blend silken tofu with other ingredients to make creamy sauces, dressings, or desserts like smoothies or puddings.

Scrambling

- Press firm tofu and crumble it into a skillet.
- Season with spices and cook over medium heat, stirring occasionally, until heated through and slightly browned.

Freezing

- Freezing tofu changes its texture, making it chewier and more porous. Press the tofu, freeze it overnight, then thaw before using in recipes like stir-fries or sandwiches for a different texture.

Braising

- Cut tofu into cubes or slices.
- Sear tofu in a hot pan with oil until golden brown on all sides.
- Add broth, soy sauce, or other braising liquid to the pan and bring to a simmer.
- Cover and cook over low heat for 20-30 minutes until tofu is tender and flavorful.

Fermenting

- Press tofu and cut it into cubes or slices.
- Prepare a brine with salt, water, and optional flavorings like garlic or herbs.
- Submerge tofu in the brine and let it ferment in a cool, dark place for several days to develop tangy flavors.

Sous Vide

- Press tofu and cut it into desired shapes.
- Place tofu in a vacuum-sealed bag with marinade or seasoning.
- Cook tofu in a sous vide water bath at the desired temperature and time for your recipe.

Cooking Methods for Tofu

Pickling

- Cut tofu into cubes or slices.
- Prepare a pickling liquid with vinegar, water, sugar, and spices of your choice.
- Place tofu in a jar or container and pour the pickling liquid over it.
- Let tofu marinate in the refrigerator for at least 24 hours before using.

Smoking

- Press tofu and cut it into large chunks.
- Prepare a smoker according to manufacturer's instructions, using wood chips of your choice.
- Place tofu on the smoker rack and smoke for 20-30 minutes, until infused with smoky flavor.

Deep-Frying

- Cut tofu into cubes or slices.
- Heat oil in a deep fryer or pot to 375°F (190°C).
- Carefully add tofu to the hot oil and fry until golden brown and crispy, about 3-5 minutes.
- Remove tofu from oil and drain on paper towels before serving.

Searing

- Press tofu and cut it into thick slices or cubes.
- Heat a non-stick skillet over medium-high heat and add a small amount of oil.
- Once the skillet is hot, add the tofu slices or cubes in a single layer.
- Let the tofu sear without moving it for 3-4 minutes, until a golden-brown crust forms on the bottom.
- Flip the tofu and sear the other side for an additional 3-4 minutes.
- Remove from heat and use in sandwiches, salads, or as a main dish with your favorite sauce or seasoning.

TOOLS AND EQUIPMENT NEEDED

1. **Cutting Tools:**
   - Chef's knife
   - Paring knife
   - Cutting board
2. **Cookware**:
   - Skillet or frying pan
   - Saucepan
   - Stockpot
   - Baking sheets or pans
   - Tofu Press
3. **Kitchen Appliances:**
   - Blender or food processor
   - Immersion blender (hand blender)
   - Slow cooker or crockpot (optional)
   - Rice cooker (optional)
4. **Measuring Tools:**
   - Measuring cups and spoons
   - Kitchen scale (optional)
5. **Food Storage:**
   - Airtight containers for storing leftovers
   - Freezer-safe containers for meal prep
6. **Utensils:**
   - Wooden spoons
   - Silicone spatulas
   - Tongs
   - Whisk

7. **Miscellaneous:**
   - Garlic press
   - Vegetable peeler
   - Can opener
   - Tongs
8. **Safety Equipment:**
   - Oven mitts or pot holders
   - Kitchen towels
9. **Specialty Items (if applicable):**
   - Dehydrator (for making dried fruits and snacks)

Spiralizer (for making vegetable noodles)

10. **Cleaning Supplies:**
   - Dish soap
   - Sponge or scrub brush
   - Dish towels

PRESSING TOFU: WHY AND HOW?

1. **Improved Texture:** Pressing tofu removes excess water, resulting in a firmer texture that holds up better during cooking.
2. **Better Flavor Absorption:** Because it has less water content, tofu can more effectively absorb marinades, sauces, and seasonings, enhancing its flavour.
3. **Prevents Sogginess:** Pressing tofu helps prevent it from becoming soggy or watery when cooked, which is especially important for dishes like stir-fries and baked tofu.

How to Press Tofu:

1. **Choose Firm or Extra-Firm Tofu**: Firm and extra-firm tofu varieties are best for pressing, as they can withstand pressure without crumbling.
2. **Wrap Tofu in Paper Towels or Cloth**: Place the block of tofu on a plate or cutting board lined with several layers of paper towels or a clean kitchen towel.
3. **Add Weight**: Place another plate or cutting board on top of the tofu and weigh it down with heavy objects like cans, a cast-iron skillet, or a tofu press. The weight helps to gently squeeze out excess moisture.
4. **Let it Press**: Allow the tofu to press for at least 15-30 minutes. Press it for up to an hour or longer for even firmer tofu.
5. **Change Paper Towels if Necessary**: If the paper towels become saturated with water during the pressing process, you may need to replace them with dry ones to continue pressing effectively.
6. **Use Pressed Tofu**: Once pressed, the tofu can be sliced, diced, marinated, or cooked according to your recipe.

TOFU

CHAPTER 2

BREAKFAST

Simple Tofu Scramble

 4 servings 20 minutes

INGREDIENTS

1 block (about 14 oz) firm tofu, drained and pressed

1 tablespoon olive oil

1/2 small onion, diced

1 bell pepper, diced

2 cloves garlic, minced

1 teaspoon turmeric

1/2 teaspoon cumin

Salt and pepper to taste

Optional toppings: chopped green onions, diced tomatoes, avocado slices, hot sauce

DIRECTIONS

1. Heat olive oil in a large skillet over medium heat.
2. Crumble the pressed tofu into the skillet, breaking it apart with a spatula.
3. Add diced onion, bell pepper, and minced garlic to the skillet. Cook until vegetables are tender, about 5-7 minutes.
4. Sprinkle turmeric and cumin over the tofu mixture and season with salt and pepper to taste. Stir well to combine, ensuring the tofu is evenly coated with spices.
5. Continue to cook for 2-3 minutes, allowing the flavours to meld together.
6. Serve hot, garnished with optional toppings like chopped green onions, diced tomatoes, avocado slices, or hot sauce.

NUTRITION INFO

Calories: 150 kcal

Protein: 10g

Fat: 10g

Carbohydrates: 7g

Fiber: 2g

Sugar: 2g

Sodium: 150mg

Crispy Baked Tofu Nuggets

 4 servings   40 minutes

INGREDIENTS

1 block (14 oz) extra-firm tofu, pressed and drained

2 tablespoons soy sauce or tamari

2 tablespoons maple syrup or honey

1 tablespoon olive oil

1 teaspoon garlic powder

1 teaspoon onion powder

1 teaspoon paprika

1/2 teaspoon salt

1/4 teaspoon black pepper

1 cup breadcrumbs (preferably panko)

Cooking spray or additional olive oil for greasing

DIRECTIONS

1. Preheat your oven to 400°F (200°C) and line a baking sheet with parchment paper or lightly grease it with cooking spray.
2. Cut the pressed tofu into small nugget-sized pieces or strips.
3. In a shallow bowl, whisk together soy sauce, maple syrup, olive oil, garlic powder, onion powder, paprika, salt, and black pepper to make the marinade.
4. Place the tofu pieces in the marinade, ensuring they are evenly coated. Let them marinate for about 10 minutes, flipping them halfway through if needed.
5. Place the breadcrumbs in another shallow bowl.
6. Coat each marinated tofu piece in breadcrumbs, pressing gently to adhere the breadcrumbs to the tofu.
7. Place the breaded tofu nuggets on the prepared baking sheet, making sure they are spaced apart.
8. Lightly spray the tops of the nuggets with cooking spray or drizzle them with a little olive oil for extra crispiness.
9. Bake in the preheated oven for 20-25 minutes, flipping halfway through, until the tofu nuggets are golden brown and crispy.
10. Once done, remove from the oven and let them cool slightly before serving.

NUTRITION INFO

Calories: 210 kcal

Total Fat: 7g

Saturated Fat: 1g

Trans Fat: 0g

Cholesterol: 0mg

Sodium: 580mg

Tofu and Vegetable Hash

 4 servings 35 minutes

INGREDIENTS

1 block (14 oz) firm tofu, drained and pressed

2 tablespoons olive oil

1 small onion, diced

2 cloves garlic, minced

1 bell pepper, diced

2 cups diced potatoes

1 teaspoon paprika

1/2 teaspoon ground cumin

Salt and pepper to taste

Fresh parsley or green onions for garnish (optional)

DIRECTIONS

1. Start by preparing the tofu. Drain the tofu and wrap it in a clean kitchen towel or paper towel. Place a heavy object on top to press out excess moisture for about 10-15 minutes. Once pressed, crumble the tofu into small pieces with your hands or a fork.

2. In a large skillet, heat olive oil over medium heat. Add diced onion and minced garlic. Sauté until onions are translucent, about 2-3 minutes.

3. Add diced bell pepper and potatoes to the skillet. Cook, stirring occasionally, until the potatoes are golden brown and cooked through about 10-12 minutes.

4. Add the crumbled tofu to the skillet, along with paprika, ground cumin, salt, and pepper. Stir well to combine all ingredients.

5. Cook for 5-7 minutes until the tofu is heated through and slightly crispy, stirring occasionally.

6. Taste and adjust seasoning if needed. Garnish with fresh parsley or green onions if desired.

7. Serve hot as a delicious breakfast or brunch dish.

NUTRITION INFO

Calories: 230 kcal

Total Fat: 12g

Saturated Fat: 2g

Cholesterol: 0mg

Sodium: 150mg

Total Carbohydrate: 21g

Dietary Fiber: 4g

Sugars: 3g

Protein: 12g

Tofu and Spinach Breakfast Sandwich

 2 servings   20 minutes

INGREDIENTS

1 block (about 14 oz) firm tofu, drained and pressed

1 tablespoon olive oil

1 teaspoon turmeric

Salt and pepper to taste

2 whole grain English muffins, split and toasted

1 cup fresh spinach leaves

2 slices vegan cheese (optional)

2 slices tomato

2 tablespoons vegan mayo

1 tablespoon Dijon mustard

DIRECTIONS

1. Slice the pressed tofu into four equal slices.
2. In a non-stick skillet, heat olive oil over medium heat.
3. Add tofu slices to the skillet and sprinkle with turmeric, salt, and pepper.
4. Cook tofu on each side for 3-4 minutes or until golden brown.
5. In the meantime, toast the English muffins until golden brown.
6. Spread vegan mayo on the bottom half of each English muffin and Dijon mustard on the top half.
7. Place a slice of tofu on the bottom half of each English muffin.
8. Top tofu with spinach leaves, tomato slices, and vegan cheese (if using).
9. Place the top half of the English muffin on each sandwich.
10. Serve immediately and enjoy!

NUTRITION INFO

Calories: 320 kcal Total

Total Fat: 17g Carbohydrates: 27g

Saturated Fat: 3g Dietary Fiber: 6g

Trans Fat: 0g Sugars: 3g

Cholesterol: 0mg Protein: 20g

Sodium: 560mg

14

Tofu Breakfast Bowl with Quinoa and Avocado

★★★★★

2 servings   30 minutes

INGREDIENTS

1 cup cooked quinoa

200g firm tofu, pressed and cubed

1 tablespoon olive oil

1/2 teaspoon garlic powder

1/2 teaspoon onion powder

Salt and pepper to taste

1 avocado, sliced

1 cup cherry tomatoes, halved

2 cups baby spinach leaves

2 tablespoons lemon juice

2 tablespoons tahini

Optional toppings: sesame seeds, red pepper flakes

DIRECTIONS

1. In a skillet, heat olive oil over medium heat. Add cubed tofu and season with garlic powder, onion powder, salt, and pepper. Cook for 5-7 minutes, or until tofu is golden brown and crispy on all sides.
2. In a large bowl, combine cooked quinoa, crispy tofu, sliced avocado, halved cherry tomatoes, and baby spinach leaves.
3. In a small bowl, whisk together lemon juice and tahini to make the dressing.
4. Drizzle the dressing over the tofu breakfast bowl and toss gently to combine.
5. Divide the mixture into two bowls and top with optional toppings like sesame seeds and red pepper flakes, if desired.
6. Serve immediately and enjoy!

NUTRITION INFO

Calories: 410 kcal

Total Fat: 26g

Saturated Fat: 4g

Trans Fat: 0g

Cholesterol: 0mg

Sodium: 140mg

CHAPTER 3

APPETIZERS AND SNACKS

Tofu Feta Cheese and Olive Tapenade Crostini

 12 serving   15 minutes

INGREDIENTS

1 block (14 oz) firm tofu, pressed and crumbled

2 tablespoons olive oil

2 tablespoons lemon juice

2 tablespoons apple cider vinegar

2 cloves garlic, minced

1 teaspoon dried oregano

Salt and pepper to taste

1 French baguette, sliced into rounds

1 cup black olives, pitted and chopped

2 tablespoons capers, chopped

2 tablespoons fresh parsley, chopped

2 tablespoons extra virgin olive oil

1 tablespoon lemon juice

Salt and pepper to taste

Fresh basil leaves, for garnish (optional)

DIRECTIONS

1. Preheat the oven to 375°F (190°C).
2. Combine the crumbled tofu, olive oil, lemon juice, apple cider vinegar, minced garlic, dried oregano, salt, and pepper in a mixing bowl. Mix well to coat the tofu evenly with the marinade. Let it marinate for at least 30 minutes or longer for better flavour.
3. Arrange the baguette slices on a baking sheet and toast them in the oven for 5-7 minutes or until they are lightly golden and crispy.
4. To make the olive tapenade, mix the chopped olives, capers, fresh parsley, extra virgin olive oil, lemon juice, salt, and pepper in another bowl.
5. To assemble the crostini, spread the marinated tofu and feta cheese on each toasted baguette slice. Top with a spoonful of olive tapenade.
6. If you'd like, please make sure to get it with fresh basil leaves and serve immediately.

NUTRITION INFO

Calories: 160 kcal	Total Carbohydrates: 17g
Total Fat: 8g	
Saturated Fat: 1g	
Trans Fat: 0g	Dietary Fiber: 2g
Cholesterol: 0mg	Sugars: 1g
Sodium: 350mg	Protein: 7g

Crispy Tofu Bites with Sweet Chili Sauce

 4 servings   35 minutes

INGREDIENTS

1 block firm tofu, pressed and cut into bite-sized cubes

1/2 cup cornstarch

1/2 teaspoon salt

1/2 teaspoon garlic powder

1/2 teaspoon paprika

1/4 teaspoon black pepper

Vegetable oil, for frying

Sweet chili sauce, for dipping

DIRECTIONS

1. Mix the cornstarch, salt, garlic powder, paprika, and black pepper in a shallow dish.
2. Coat each tofu cube with the cornstarch mixture, shaking off any excess.
3. Heat vegetable oil in a large skillet over medium-high heat.
4. Fry the tofu cubes in batches until golden brown and crispy, about 2-3 minutes per side.
5. Remove tofu from the skillet and drain on paper towels.
6. Serve the crispy tofu bites with sweet chilli sauce for dipping.

NUTRITION INFO

Calories: 220

Fat: 9g

Carbohydrates: 25g

Fiber: 1g

Protein: 11g

Sugar: 6g

Sodium: 460mg

18

Tofu Spring Rolls

 8 servings 30 minutes

INGREDIENTS

8 rice paper wrappers

1 block extra-firm tofu, pressed and sliced into thin strips

1 cup shredded carrots

1 cup shredded cabbage

1 cucumber, julienned

1 avocado, thinly sliced

1/4 cup fresh mint leaves

1/4 cup fresh cilantro leaves

1/4 cup chopped peanuts (optional)

Sweet chili sauce or peanut sauce for dipping

DIRECTIONS

1. Prepare all the ingredients and arrange them in separate bowls for easy assembly.
2. Fill a shallow dish with warm water. Dip one rice paper wrapper into the water for 15-20 seconds until it becomes pliable.
3. Place the softened wrapper on a clean surface. In the centre of the wrapper, arrange a few strips of tofu, carrots, cabbage, cucumber, avocado, mint leaves, and cilantro leaves.
4. Fold the bottom of the wrapper over the filling, then fold in the sides and roll tightly to enclose the filling completely.
5. Repeat with the remaining wrappers and filling ingredients.
6. Serve the spring rolls with sweet chilli sauce or peanut sauce for dipping. If desired, sprinkle with chopped peanuts.

NUTRITION INFO

Calories: 180

Total Fat: 8g

Saturated Fat: 1g

Cholesterol: 0mg

Sodium: 180mg

Tofu Stuffed Mushrooms

★★★★★

4 servings   30 minutes

INGREDIENTS

16 large mushrooms, stems removed and reserved

200g firm tofu, drained and crumbled

1 tablespoon olive oil

2 cloves garlic, minced

1/4 cup breadcrumbs

1/4 cup grated vegan cheese (optional)

2 tablespoons chopped fresh parsley

Salt and pepper to taste

Cooking spray

DIRECTIONS

1. Preheat your oven to 375°F (190°C). Lightly grease a baking dish with cooking spray.

2. Place the mushroom caps in the prepared baking dish, gill side up.

3. In a skillet, heat the olive oil over medium heat. Add the minced garlic and sauté for 1-2 minutes until fragrant.

4. Chop the reserved mushroom stems finely and add them to the skillet. Cook for another 3-4 minutes until softened.

5. Add the crumbled tofu to the skillet and cook for 3-4 minutes, stirring occasionally, until heated.

6. Remove the skillet from the heat and stir in the breadcrumbs, grated vegan cheese (if using), chopped parsley, salt, and pepper. Mix until well combined.

7. Spoon the tofu mixture into the mushroom caps, pressing down gently to fill each cap.

8. Bake in the oven for 15-20 minutes or until the mushrooms are tender and the stuffing is golden brown.

9. Serve hot as an appetizer or side dish.

NUTRITION INFO

Calories: 135 kcal

Total Fat: 7g

Saturated Fat: 1g

Trans Fat: 0g

Cholesterol: 0mg

Sodium: 162mg

Total Carbohydrates: 11g

Dietary Fiber: 2g

Sugars: 2g

Protein: 8g

Tofu and Veggie Sushi Rolls

★★★★★

4 servings   30 minutes

INGREDIENTS

1 cup sushi rice

2 cups water

2 tablespoons rice vinegar

1 tablespoon sugar

½ teaspoon salt

4 sheets nori (seaweed)

1 block extra-firm tofu, pressed and sliced into strips

1 carrot, julienned

1 cucumber, julienned

1 avocado, sliced

Soy sauce, for dipping

Pickled ginger and wasabi, for serving (optional)

DIRECTIONS

1. Rinse the sushi rice in a fine mesh strainer until the water clears. In a medium saucepan, combine the rice and water. Bring to a boil, then reduce the heat to low, cover, and simmer for 18-20 minutes or until the rice is tender and the water is absorbed.

2. Mix the rice vinegar, sugar, and salt in a small bowl until dissolved. Gently fold the vinegar mixture into the cooked rice.

3. Place a nori sheet on a bamboo sushi mat or a clean kitchen towel. With wet hands, spread a thin layer of rice evenly over the nori, leaving about 1 inch of space at the top.

4. Arrange the tofu strips, carrot, cucumber, and avocado along the bottom edge of the rice.

5. Roll the sushi tightly from the bottom, using the mat or towel to help shape it. Moisten the top edge of the nori with water to seal the roll.

6. Repeat with the remaining ingredients.

7. Using a sharp knife, slice each roll into 6-8 pieces.

8. Serve the sushi rolls with soy sauce, pickled ginger, and wasabi if you'd like.

NUTRITION INFO

Calories: 220   Total

Total Fat: 8g   Carbohydrate: 31g

Saturated Fat: 1g Dietary Fiber: 5g

Cholesterol: 0mg Sugars: 4g

Sodium: 250mg   Protein: 7g

CHAPTER 4

Soups and Salads

Tofu and Vegetable Miso Soup

 4 servings 30 minutes

INGREDIENTS

4 cups vegetable broth

1 block (about 14 oz) firm tofu, cubed

1 cup sliced mushrooms (shiitake, button, or your choice)

1 cup chopped bok choy or spinach

1/2 cup diced carrots

1/4 cup diced green onions

3 tablespoons miso paste (white or yellow)

2 tablespoons soy sauce or tamari

1 tablespoon sesame oil

1 tablespoon grated ginger

2 cloves garlic, minced

Optional toppings: sliced green onions, sesame seeds, nori strips

DIRECTIONS

1. In a large pot, heat sesame oil over medium heat. Add minced garlic, grated ginger, and sauté for 1-2 minutes until fragrant.
2. Add sliced mushrooms and diced carrots to the pot and cook for 3-4 minutes until slightly softened.
3. Pour in vegetable broth and bring to a gentle boil. Reduce heat to low.
4. Whisk together miso paste and soy sauce until smooth in a small bowl.
5. Add cubed tofu and chopped bok choy (or spinach) to the pot, and simmer for another 3-4 minutes until the vegetables are tender and the tofu is heated through.
6. Remove the pot from heat. Stir in the miso-soy mixture until well combined.
7. Taste and adjust seasoning if needed.
8. If desired, serve hot, garnished with sliced green onions, sesame seeds, and nori strips.

NUTRITION INFO

Calories: 180

Total Fat: 9g

Saturated Fat: 1.5g

Trans Fat: 0g

23

Tofu Stir-Fry with Vegetables

★★★★★

 4 servings 30 minutes

INGREDIENTS

14 oz (400g) firm tofu, drained and cubed

2 tablespoons soy sauce (or tamari for gluten-free option)

1 tablespoon sesame oil

2 cloves garlic, minced

1 teaspoon ginger, minced

1 red bell pepper, sliced

1 yellow bell pepper, sliced

1 cup broccoli florets

1 cup snap peas

1 carrot, julienned

2 green onions, chopped

For the Sauce:

1/4 cup soy sauce (or tamari)

2 tablespoons rice vinegar

1 tablespoon maple syrup or brown sugar

1 teaspoon cornstarch

DIRECTIONS

1. Marinate the cubed tofu in a bowl with two tablespoons of soy sauce for about 10 minutes.
2. In another bowl, whisk together the sauce ingredients: 1/4 cup soy sauce, rice vinegar, maple syrup or brown sugar, and cornstarch. Set aside.
3. Heat sesame oil in a large skillet or wok over medium-high heat. Add minced garlic and ginger, and stir-fry for 30 seconds until fragrant.
4. Add marinated tofu to the skillet. Cook for 5-7 minutes, stirring occasionally, until tofu is golden brown.
5. Add sliced bell peppers, broccoli florets, snap peas, and julienned carrot to the skillet. Stir-fry for another 3-5 minutes until vegetables are tender-crisp.
6. Pour the sauce over the tofu and vegetables. Stir well to coat everything evenly. Cook for an additional 1-2 minutes until the sauce thickens.
7. Garnish with chopped green onions. Serve hot cooked rice or noodles.

NUTRITION INFO

Calories: 350	Total
Total Fat: 12g	Carbohydrates: 25g
Saturated Fat: 4g	Dietary Fiber: 6g
Cholesterol: 90mg	Sugars: 8g
Sodium: 800mg	Protein: 32g

24

Tofu Caesar Salad with Homemade Dressing

★★★★★

4 servings   15 minutes

INGREDIENTS

1 block (14 oz) firm tofu, pressed and cubed

1 head romaine lettuce, washed and chopped

1 cup cherry tomatoes, halved

1/4 cup croutons

2 tablespoons olive oil

2 cloves garlic, minced

1 teaspoon Dijon mustard

2 tablespoons lemon juice

2 tablespoons nutritional yeast

Salt and pepper to taste

Optional: vegan parmesan cheese for garnish

DIRECTIONS

1. In a small bowl, whisk together olive oil, minced garlic, Dijon mustard, lemon juice, nutritional yeast, salt, and pepper until well combined.

For the Salad:

1. Combine chopped romaine lettuce, cherry tomatoes, and cubed tofu in a large salad bowl.
2. Pour the homemade dressing over the salad and toss gently to coat evenly.
3. Please just top the salad with croutons and vegan parmesan cheese if you'd like.

NUTRITION INFO

Calories: 220 kcal

Protein: 12g

Fat: 14g

Carbohydrates: 14g

Fiber: 6g

Sugar: 3g

Tofu and Edamame Salad with Ginger-Soy Dressing

 4 servings | 20 minutes

INGREDIENTS

1 block (14 oz) firm tofu, drained and cubed

1 cup shelled edamame, cooked

2 cups mixed salad greens

1 carrot, julienned

1 red bell pepper, thinly sliced

2 green onions, chopped

1 tablespoon sesame seeds (optional, for garnish)

For the Ginger-Soy Dressing:

2 tablespoons soy sauce

1 tablespoon rice vinegar

1 tablespoon sesame oil

1 tablespoon freshly grated ginger

1 garlic clove, minced

DIRECTIONS

1. Whisk together all the ingredients for the ginger-soy dressing in a small bowl. Set aside.
2. Combine the cubed tofu, cooked edamame, mixed salad greens, julienned carrot, sliced red bell pepper, and chopped green onions in a large salad bowl.
3. Pour the ginger-soy dressing over the salad and toss gently to coat everything evenly.
4. Sprinkle sesame seeds over the salad for garnish, if desired.
5. Serve immediately or refrigerate until ready to serve.

NUTRITION INFO

Calories: 220 kcal

Total Fat: 12g

Saturated Fat: 2g

Trans Fat: 0g

Creamy Tofu Tomato Soup

 4 servings 3 minutes

★★★★★

INGREDIENTS

1 tablespoon olive oil

1 onion, chopped

2 cloves garlic, minced

1 (28-ounce) can crushed tomatoes

1 (14-ounce) package firm tofu, drained and cubed

2 cups vegetable broth

1 teaspoon dried basil

1 teaspoon dried oregano

Salt and pepper, to taste

1/2 cup coconut milk (or any non-dairy milk)

Fresh basil leaves, for garnish (optional)

DIRECTIONS

1. In a large pot, heat the olive oil over medium heat. Add the chopped onion, minced garlic, and sauté until softened, about 5 minutes.

2. Add the crushed tomatoes, cubed tofu, vegetable broth, dried basil, and oregano to the pot—season with salt and pepper to taste.

3. Bring the soup to a simmer, then reduce the heat to low. Let it simmer for 15-20 minutes, stirring occasionally, to allow the flavors to meld together.

4. Blend the soup until smooth and creamy using an immersion or regular blender.

5. Stir in the coconut milk until well combined. Taste and adjust seasoning if needed.

6. Serve the soup hot, garnished with fresh basil leaves if desired.

NUTRITION INFO

Calories: 195 kcal

Total Fat: 11g

Saturated Fat: 5g

Trans Fat: 0g

Cholesterol: 0mg

Sodium: 622mg

Total Carbohydrates: 17g

CHAPTER 5

MAIN DISHES

Tofu Tikka Masala

 4 servings 25 minutes

INGREDIENTS

14 oz (400g) extra-firm tofu, pressed and cubed

1 cup plain yogurt (use dairy-free yogurt for vegan option)

2 tablespoons tikka masala paste

2 tablespoons vegetable oil

1 onion, finely chopped

2 cloves garlic, minced

1-inch piece of ginger, grated

1 bell pepper, diced

1 can (14 oz) diced tomatoes

1 teaspoon ground cumin

1 teaspoon ground coriander

1 teaspoon paprika

Salt and pepper to taste

Fresh cilantro, chopped (for garnish)

NUTRITION INFO

Calories: 320 kcal

Total Fat: 18g

Saturated Fat: 3g

Cholesterol: 2mg

Sodium: 420mg

DIRECTIONS

1. Mix the yoghurt and tikka masala paste in a bowl until well combined. Add the cubed tofu and toss until evenly coated—Marinate for at least 30 minutes or overnight for the best flavour.

2. Heat one tablespoon of oil in a large skillet over medium-high heat. Add the marinated tofu cubes and cook until browned on all sides, about 5-7 minutes. Remove the tofu from the skillet and set aside.

3. In the same skillet, heat the remaining tablespoon of oil. Add the chopped onion, garlic, and ginger. Sauté until the onion is soft and translucent, about 5 minutes.

4. Add the diced bell pepper to the skillet and cook for 2-3 minutes.

5. Stir in the diced tomatoes, cumin, coriander, paprika, salt, and pepper. Bring the mixture to a simmer and cook for about 10 minutes, allowing the flavours to meld.

6. Return the cooked tofu to the skillet and stir until it is heated and coated in the sauce.

7. Serve the tofu tikka masala hot over cooked rice or with naan bread. Before serving, garnish with chopped cilantro.

General Tso's Tofu

 4 serving   40 minutes

INGREDIENTS

1 block (14 oz) extra-firm tofu, drained and pressed

3 tablespoons cornstarch

2 tablespoons vegetable oil

3 cloves garlic, minced

1 tablespoon fresh ginger, minced

1/4 cup low-sodium soy sauce

3 tablespoons hoisin sauce

2 tablespoons rice vinegar

2 tablespoons brown sugar

1 teaspoon sesame oil

1/4 teaspoon red pepper flakes (optional)

2 green onions, sliced (for garnish)

DIRECTIONS

1. Preheat your oven to 400°F (200°C).
2. Cut the tofu into bite-sized cubes and toss them with cornstarch until evenly coated.
3. Place the coated tofu cubes on a baking sheet lined with parchment paper or a silicone mat. Bake for 25 minutes, flipping halfway through, until crispy.
4. While the tofu is baking, prepare the sauce. Whisk together the soy sauce, hoisin sauce, rice vinegar, brown sugar, sesame oil, and red pepper flakes in a small bowl. Set aside.
5. Heat the vegetable oil over medium-high heat in a large skillet or wok. Add the minced garlic and ginger, and sauté for 1-2 minutes until fragrant.
6. Add the baked tofu to the skillet and pour the sauce over the tofu. Stir to coat the tofu evenly in the sauce. Cook for 2-3 minutes until the sauce thickens and coats the tofu.
7. Serve the General Tso's tofu hot overcooked rice garnished with sliced green onions.

NUTRITION INFO

Calories: 280 kcal

Total Fat: 14g

Saturated Fat: 2g

Trans Fat: 0g

Cholesterol: 0mg

Sodium: 640mg

Tofu and Vegetable Stir-Fry with Peanut Sauce

 4 servings 30 minutes

INGREDIENTS

1 block (14 oz) extra-firm tofu, pressed and cubed

2 tablespoons soy sauce

2 tablespoons sesame oil

1 tablespoon cornstarch

2 tablespoons vegetable oil

2 cloves garlic, minced

1 tablespoon ginger, minced

1 bell pepper, thinly sliced

1 cup broccoli florets

1 cup snow peas, trimmed

1 carrot, julienned

4 green onions, sliced

Cooked rice or noodles, for serving

Peanut Sauce:

1/4 cup creamy peanut butter

2 tablespoons soy sauce

1 tablespoon maple syrup or honey

1 tablespoon rice vinegar

1 teaspoon sesame oil

1 clove garlic, minced

1 teaspoon grated ginger

2-4 tablespoons water (to thin as needed)

DIRECTIONS

1. Mix the soy sauce, sesame oil, and cornstarch in a medium bowl. Add the cubed tofu and toss until evenly coated. Let it marinate for about 10 minutes.

2. In a small bowl, whisk together all the ingredients for the peanut sauce until smooth. Set aside.

3. Heat vegetable oil in a large skillet or wok over medium-high heat. Add the marinated tofu and cook until golden brown and crispy on all sides, about 5-7 minutes. Remove tofu from the skillet and set aside.

4. In the same skillet, add a bit more oil if needed. Add minced garlic and ginger, and stir-fry for 30 seconds until fragrant.

5. Add bell pepper, broccoli florets, snow peas, and julienned carrot to the skillet. Stir-fry for 3-4 minutes until vegetables are tender-crisp.

6. Return the cooked tofu to the skillet. Pour the peanut sauce over the tofu and vegetables. Stir well to combine and coat everything in the sauce. Cook for another 1-2 minutes until heated through.

7. Remove from heat and sprinkle sliced green onions on top. Serve the tofu and vegetable stir-fry over cooked rice or noodles.

31

Tofu Pad Thai

 4 servings 30 minutes

INGREDIENTS

8 oz rice noodles

2 tbsp vegetable oil

1 block (14 oz) firm tofu, drained and cubed

2 cloves garlic, minced

2 eggs, lightly beaten

1 cup bean sprouts

1 red bell pepper, thinly sliced

3 green onions, chopped

1/4 cup chopped peanuts

Lime wedges, for serving

Fresh cilantro, for garnish

For the Sauce:

3 tbsp soy sauce

2 tbsp tamarind paste

2 tbsp brown sugar

1 tbsp rice vinegar

1 tsp Sriracha sauce (optional)

NUTRITION INFO

Calories: 380 kcal

Protein: 15g

Fat: 14g

Carbohydrates: 50g

Fiber: 4g

DIRECTIONS

1. Cook the rice noodles according to package instructions. Drain and set aside.

2. In a small bowl, whisk together the soy sauce, tamarind paste, brown sugar, rice vinegar, and Sriracha sauce to make the sauce. Set aside.

3. Heat one tablespoon of vegetable oil in a large pan over medium-high heat. Add the tofu cubes and cook until golden brown on all sides, about 5-7 minutes. Remove the tofu from the pan and set aside.

4. In the same pan, heat the remaining tablespoon of vegetable oil. Add the minced garlic and cook for about 30 seconds or until fragrant.

5. Push the garlic to the side of the pan and pour the beaten eggs into the space. Scramble the eggs until fully cooked, then mix them with the garlic.

6. Add the cooked rice noodles, tofu, bean sprouts, bell pepper, green onions, and sauce to the pan. Stir everything until well combined and heated, about 3-5 minutes.

7. Remove the pan from heat and sprinkle chopped peanuts over the top.

8. Serve the tofu pad Thai hot, garnished with lime wedges and fresh cilantro.

Tofu and Broccoli in Garlic Sauce

 4 servings   30 minutes

INGREDIENTS

1 block (14 oz) extra firm tofu, drained and pressed

2 cups broccoli florets

3 cloves garlic, minced

2 tablespoons soy sauce

1 tablespoon hoisin sauce

1 tablespoon rice vinegar

1 tablespoon sesame oil

1 tablespoon cornstarch

2 tablespoons water

1 tablespoon vegetable oil

Salt and pepper, to taste

Cooked rice, for serving

Sesame seeds and sliced green onions, for garnish (optional)

DIRECTIONS

1. Cut the pressed tofu into cubes and set aside.
2. To make the sauce, whisk together soy sauce, hoisin sauce, rice vinegar, sesame oil, cornstarch, and water in a small bowl. Set aside.
3. Heat vegetable oil in a large skillet or wok over medium-high heat. Add minced garlic and cook for 1 minute until fragrant.
4. Add tofu cubes to the skillet and cook until golden brown on all sides, about 5-7 minutes. Remove tofu from the skillet and set aside.
5. In the same skillet, add broccoli florets and cook for 3-4 minutes until slightly tender.
6. Return the tofu to the skillet with the broccoli. Pour the sauce over the tofu and broccoli, stirring well to coat.
7. Cook for 2-3 minutes, allowing the sauce to thicken and the flavors to combine.
8. Season with salt and pepper to taste.
9. Serve hot cooked rice garnished with sesame seeds and sliced green onions if desired.

NUTRITION INFO

- Calories: 250 kcal
- Protein: 16g
- Carbohydrates: 14g
- Fat: 14g
- Fiber: 4g
-

TOFU

CHAPTER 6

DESSERTS

Tofu Coconut Pudding

 4 servings 10 minutes

INGREDIENTS

1 (12-ounce) package silken tofu, drained

1 cup coconut milk

1/4 cup maple syrup or sweetener of choice

1 teaspoon vanilla extract

Pinch of salt

Toasted coconut flakes, for garnish (optional)

DIRECTIONS

1. Combine the silken tofu, coconut milk, maple syrup, vanilla extract, and salt in a blender or food processor. Blend until smooth and creamy.
2. Taste the mixture and adjust sweetness if desired by adding more maple syrup.
3. Pour the mixture into serving cups or ramekins.
4. Refrigerate for at least 2 hours or until set.
5. Before serving, garnish with toasted coconut flakes if desired.
6. Enjoy chilled!

NUTRITION INFO

Calories: 230 kcal

Total Fat: 13g

Saturated Fat: 9g

Trans Fat: 0g

Cholesterol: 0mg

Sodium: 20mg

Total Carbohydrates: 28g

Dietary Fiber: 6g

Sugars: 19g

Protein: 4g

Vegan Tofu Cheesecake

 8 servings 20 minutes

INGREDIENTS

1 1/2 cups graham cracker crumbs (or cookie crumbs of choice)

1/4 cup coconut oil, melted

2 tablespoons maple syrup

For the filling:

1 (14-ounce) block firm tofu, drained

1/2 cup coconut cream

1/4 cup lemon juice

1/4 cup maple syrup

1 teaspoon vanilla extract

2 tablespoons cornstarch

For the topping:

Fresh berries or fruit of choice (optional)

DIRECTIONS

1. Preheat the oven to 350°F (175°C). Grease a 9-inch pie dish or springform pan.
2. In a mixing bowl, combine the graham cracker crumbs, melted coconut oil, and maple syrup for the crust. Press the mixture firmly into the bottom of the prepared pan.
3. Bake the crust for 10 minutes, then remove from the oven and let it cool while you prepare the filling.
4. In a food processor or blender, combine the drained tofu, coconut cream, lemon juice, maple syrup, vanilla extract, and cornstarch. Blend until smooth and creamy.
5. Pour the filling mixture over the cooled crust, spreading it evenly with a spatula.
6. Place the cheesecake in the refrigerator to chill for at least 4 hours, or until set.
7. Once chilled and set, remove the cheesecake from the pan, slice into 8 pieces, and serve with fresh berries or fruit if desired.

NUTRITION INFO

Calories: 200 kcal

Total Fat: 15g

Saturated Fat: 2g

Sodium: 5mg

Total Carbohydrates: 20g

36

Tofu Chocolate Mousse

 4 servings 15 minutes

INGREDIENTS

1 block (14 ounces) firm tofu, drained

1/3 cup cocoa powder

1/3 cup maple syrup or agave nectar

1 teaspoon vanilla extract

Pinch of salt

Optional toppings: fresh berries, shaved chocolate, whipped coconut cream

DIRECTIONS

1. In a food processor or blender, combine the tofu, cocoa powder, maple syrup or agave nectar, vanilla extract, and a pinch of salt.
2. Blend the mixture until smooth and creamy, scraping down the sides of the processor or blender as needed.
3. Taste the mousse and adjust sweetness or cocoa flavour if desired by adding more sweetener or cocoa powder.
4. Transfer the chocolate mousse to serving bowls or glasses.
5. Chill in the refrigerator for at least 1 hour before serving.
6. Optionally, garnish with fresh berries, shaved chocolate, or whipped coconut cream before serving.

NUTRITION INFO

Calories: 150

Total Fat: 1g

Saturated Fat: 0g

Cholesterol: 0mg

Sodium: 5mg

Total Carbohydrates: 40g

Dietary Fiber: 6g

Sugars: 30g

Protein: 1g

Tofu Pumpkin Pie

 8 servings 1 hour 5 minutes

INGREDIENTS

1 (15 oz) can pumpkin puree

1 (12 oz) package silken tofu, drained

3/4 cup brown sugar

1 teaspoon vanilla extract

1 teaspoon ground cinnamon

1/2 teaspoon ground ginger

1/4 teaspoon ground nutmeg

1/4 teaspoon ground cloves

1/4 teaspoon salt

1 (9-inch) unbaked pie crust (store-bought or homemade)

DIRECTIONS

1. Preheat your oven to 425°F (220°C).
2. Combine the pumpkin puree, silken tofu, brown sugar, vanilla extract, cinnamon, ginger, nutmeg, cloves, and salt in a blender or food processor. Blend until smooth and well combined.
3. Pour the pumpkin mixture into the unbaked pie crust, spreading it evenly.
4. Place the pie in the preheated oven and bake for 15 minutes.
5. After 15 minutes, reduce the oven temperature to 350°F (175°C) and continue baking for 35 minutes, or until the filling is set and a toothpick inserted into the centre comes out clean.
6. Remove the pie from the oven and let it cool completely before serving.
7. Once cooled, slice the pie into 8 equal servings.
8. Serve the tofu pumpkin pie slices on plates and optionally top with whipped cream or a sprinkle of cinnamon before serving.

NUTRITION INFO

Calories: 100 kcal

Total Fat: 0g

Cholesterol: 0mg

Sodium: 0mg

Total Carbohydrates: 26g

Dietary Fiber: 3g

Sugars: 20g

Protein: 1g

Tofu Berry Parfait

2 serving   15 minutes

INGREDIENTS

1 cup firm tofu, drained and cubed

1 tablespoon maple syrup or agave nectar

1 teaspoon vanilla extract

1 cup mixed berries (such as strawberries, blueberries, raspberries)

1/4 cup granola (optional, for topping)

Fresh mint leaves, for garnish (optional)

DIRECTIONS

1. In a blender or food processor, combine the firm tofu, maple syrup or agave nectar, and vanilla extract. Blend until smooth and creamy.
2. In serving glasses or bowls, layer the tofu mixture with mixed berries, starting with a layer of tofu mixture at the bottom.
3. Continue layering with berries and tofu mixture until the glasses or bowls are filled.
4. Top each parfait with a sprinkle of granola, if desired, and garnish with fresh mint leaves.
5. Serve immediately, or refrigerate until ready to serve.

NUTRITION INFO

Calories: 155 kcal

Total Fat: 13g

Saturated Fat: 4g

Sodium: 48mg

Total Carbohydrates: 8g

Dietary Fiber: 2g

Sugars: 4g

Protein: 4g

TOFU

CHAPTER 7

GRILLING AND BBQ

Grilled Tofu Skewers with Vegetables

★★★★★

🍴 4 servings   🕐 30 minutes

INGREDIENTS

1 block (14 oz) firm tofu, pressed and cut into cubes

1 red bell pepper, cut into chunks

1 green bell pepper, cut into chunks

1 yellow bell pepper, cut into chunks

1 red onion, cut into chunks

8 cherry tomatoes

2 tablespoons olive oil

2 cloves garlic, minced

2 tablespoons soy sauce or tamari

1 tablespoon maple syrup or honey

1 tablespoon rice vinegar

1 teaspoon smoked paprika

Salt and pepper to taste

Wooden or metal skewers

DIRECTIONS

1. If using wooden skewers, soak them in water for at least 30 minutes to prevent burning during grilling.
2. To make the marinade, whisk together olive oil, minced garlic, soy sauce, maple syrup, rice vinegar, smoked paprika, salt, and pepper in a small bowl.
3. Thread the tofu cubes, bell peppers, red onion chunks, and cherry tomatoes onto the skewers, alternating the ingredients.
4. Place the skewers in a shallow dish and pour the marinade over them, evenly coating all pieces. Let them marinate for at least 10 minutes, or refrigerate for 1 hour for more flavour.
5. Preheat the grill to medium-high heat. Brush the grill grates lightly with oil to prevent sticking.
6. Place the tofu skewers on the grill and cook for about 4–5 minutes on each side until the tofu is lightly charred and the vegetables are tender, turning occasionally and basting with any remaining marinade.
7. Once cooked, remove the skewers from the grill and let them cool slightly before serving.
8. Please make sure to serve the grilled tofu skewers with vegetables hot, garnished with chopped fresh herbs like parsley or cilantro if you want to.

BBQ Tofu Sandwiches

★★★★★

 4 servings 35 minutes

INGREDIENTS

1 block extra-firm tofu, pressed and sliced into ½-inch thick rectangles

½ cup barbecue sauce

2 tablespoons olive oil

1 teaspoon garlic powder

1 teaspoon smoked paprika

½ teaspoon onion powder

Salt and pepper to taste

4 hamburger buns

Optional toppings: sliced red onion, lettuce, tomato, pickles

DIRECTIONS

1. Preheat your oven to 375°F (190°C). Line a baking sheet with parchment paper or lightly grease it.
2. Whisk together the barbecue sauce, olive oil, garlic powder, smoked paprika, onion powder, salt, and pepper in a small bowl.
3. Place the tofu slices on the prepared baking sheet. Brush both sides of each tofu slice generously with the barbecue sauce mixture.
4. Bake the tofu in the preheated oven for 20-25 minutes, flipping halfway through, until the tofu is golden and crispy on the edges.
5. While the tofu is baking, lightly toast the hamburger buns in a toaster or oven.
6. Once the tofu is done, assemble the sandwiches by placing a few slices on each bottom bun. Add any desired toppings, such as sliced red onion, lettuce, tomato, or pickles. Top with the remaining bun halves.
7. Serve the BBQ tofu sandwiches immediately.

Tofu and Pineapple Teriyaki Kabobs

 4 servings 30 minutes

INGREDIENTS

1 block extra firm tofu, pressed and cut into 1-inch cubes

1 cup pineapple chunks

1 red bell pepper, cut into chunks

1 green bell pepper, cut into chunks

1 red onion, cut into chunks

½ cup teriyaki sauce

2 tablespoons soy sauce

2 tablespoons olive oil

2 cloves garlic, minced

1 teaspoon ginger, grated

Wooden or metal skewers

DIRECTIONS

1. In a small bowl, whisk together the teriyaki sauce, soy sauce, olive oil, minced garlic, and grated ginger to make the marinade.
2. Place the tofu cubes in a shallow dish and pour half of the marinade over them. Allow tofu to marinate for at least 15 minutes or longer.
3. Preheat the grill or grill pan to medium-high heat.
4. Thread marinated tofu, pineapple chunks, red bell pepper, green bell pepper, and red onion onto skewers, alternating between tofu and vegetables.
5. Brush the skewers with the remaining marinade.
6. Grill the kabobs for about 5 minutes on each side or until the tofu and vegetables are lightly charred and cooked through.
7. Serve hot, garnished with chopped green onions or sesame seeds if desired.

NUTRITION INFO

Calories: 240 kcal

Protein: 12g

Fat: 10g

Carbohydrates: 25g

Fiber: 4g

Sugar: 16g

Sodium: 860mg

Tofu BBQ Ribs

 4 servings 50 mins

INGREDIENTS

1 block extra-firm tofu, pressed and drained

1/2 cup barbecue sauce

2 tablespoons soy sauce

2 tablespoons maple syrup

1 tablespoon olive oil

1 teaspoon smoked paprika

1/2 teaspoon garlic powder

1/2 teaspoon onion powder

Salt and pepper to taste

Optional: chopped green onions and sesame seeds for garnish

NUTRITION INFO

Calories: 220 kcal

Protein: 11g

Fat: 10g

Carbohydrates: 23g

Fiber: 2g

Sugar: 16g

DIRECTIONS

1. Preheat your oven to 375°F (190°C). Line a baking sheet with parchment paper or lightly grease it.

2. Cut the pressed tofu block into rectangular strips resembling ribs.

3. Whisk together barbecue sauce, soy sauce, maple syrup, olive oil, smoked paprika, garlic powder, onion powder, salt, and pepper in a bowl.

4. Place the tofu ribs in a shallow dish and pour the marinade over them, ensuring they are evenly coated. Let them marinate for at least 15 minutes or up to overnight in the refrigerator for more flavor.

5. Arrange the marinated tofu ribs on the prepared baking sheet and bake in the preheated oven for 25-30 minutes, flipping halfway through, until the tofu is golden and slightly crispy.

6. Once done, remove from the oven and brush the tofu ribs with any remaining marinade for extra flavour.

7. Serve hot tofu BBQ ribs, garnished with chopped green onions and sesame seeds if desired.

Grilled Tofu Steaks with Chimichurri Sauce

★★★★★

🍴 4 servings   🕐 25 minutes

INGREDIENTS

1 block (14 oz) firm tofu, drained and pressed
2 tablespoons olive oil
Salt and pepper, to taste

Chimichurri Sauce:

1 cup fresh parsley, chopped
1/4 cup fresh cilantro, chopped
3 cloves garlic, minced
1/4 cup red wine vinegar
1/2 cup olive oil
1/2 teaspoon red pepper flakes

DIRECTIONS

1. Preheat the grill to medium-high heat.
2. Cut the tofu block into 4 equal-sized steaks.
3. Brush both sides of the tofu steaks with olive oil and season with salt and pepper.
4. Grill the tofu steaks for 4-5 minutes per side, or until grill marks appear and the tofu is heated through.
5. While the tofu is grilling, prepare the chimichurri sauce. In a bowl, combine the parsley, cilantro, garlic, red wine vinegar, olive oil, red pepper flakes, salt, and pepper. Mix well.
6. Serve the grilled tofu steaks with the chimichurri sauce drizzled on top.

NUTRITION INFO

Calories: 280 kcal
Protein: 10g
Fat: 24g
Carbohydrates: 6g
Fiber: 2g
Sugar: 1g
Sodium: 15mg

TOFU

CHAPTER 8

WRAPS AND ROLLS

Tofu Caesar Wraps

 4 servings 25 minutes

INGREDIENTS

1 block firm tofu, pressed and sliced into strips

4 large whole wheat tortillas

2 cups chopped romaine lettuce

1/2 cup cherry tomatoes, halved

1/4 cup grated vegan parmesan cheese

Caesar dressing (store-bought or homemade)

Salt and pepper to taste

DIRECTIONS

1. Preheat the oven to 375°F (190°C).
2. Place the tofu strips on a baking sheet lined with parchment paper—season with salt and pepper.
3. Bake the tofu for 20-25 minutes or until golden and crispy.
4. Warm the tortillas in a dry skillet or microwave for a few seconds to make them more pliable.
5. Spread a generous amount of Caesar dressing onto each tortilla.
6. Arrange a handful of chopped romaine lettuce on top of the dressing.
7. Place a few slices of baked tofu on the lettuce.
8. Add cherry tomatoes and sprinkle vegan parmesan cheese over the tofu.
9. Roll up the tortillas tightly, tucking in the sides as you go.
10. Slice each wrap in half diagonally and serve immediately.

NUTRITION INFO

Calories: 120

Total Fat: 7g

Saturated Fat: 1g

Cholesterol: 0mg

Sodium: 10mg

Total Carbohydrate: 14g

Dietary Fiber: 4g

Sugars: 7g

Protein: 3g

Tofu and Black Bean Burritos

 4 servings   20 minutes

INGREDIENTS

1 block (14 oz) firm tofu, drained and pressed

1 tablespoon olive oil

1 small onion, diced

2 cloves garlic, minced

1 teaspoon ground cumin

1 teaspoon chili powder

1/2 teaspoon paprika

Salt and pepper to taste

1 can (15 oz) black beans, drained and rinsed

1/2 cup corn kernels (fresh, frozen, or canned)

1/4 cup chopped fresh cilantro

4 large flour tortillas

Optional toppings: shredded cheese, diced tomatoes, avocado slices, salsa, sour cream

DIRECTIONS

1. Heat olive oil in a large skillet over medium heat. Crumble the tofu into the skillet and cook for 5-7 minutes, stirring occasionally, until lightly browned.

2. Add diced onion and minced garlic to the skillet with the tofu. Cook for an additional 2-3 minutes until the onion is softened.

3. Stir in ground cumin, chili powder, paprika, salt, and pepper. Cook for another minute until the spices are fragrant.

4. Add black beans and corn to the skillet. Cook for 3-4 minutes, stirring occasionally, until heated through.

5. Remove the skillet from heat and stir in chopped cilantro.

6. Warm the flour tortillas in a separate skillet or the microwave.

7. Spoon the tofu and black bean mixture onto each tortilla. Add toppings such as shredded cheese, diced tomatoes, avocado slices, salsa, and sour cream.

8. Roll up the tortillas into burritos, folding in the sides as you go.

9. Serve immediately and enjoy!

Tofu and Avocado Sushi Burrito

 2 servings 20 minutes

INGREDIENTS

2 large seaweed sheets (nori)

1 cup cooked sushi rice

200g firm tofu, sliced into thin strips

1 avocado, sliced

1/2 cucumber, julienned

1/2 carrot, julienned

2 tablespoons rice vinegar

1 tablespoon sugar

1 teaspoon salt

Soy sauce, for serving

Pickled ginger, for serving

Wasabi, for serving

NUTRITION INFO

Calories: 230

Total Fat: 20g

    Saturated Fat: 17g

    Trans Fat: 0g

Cholesterol: 0mg

Sodium: 300mg

Total Carbohydrates: 10g

    Dietary Fiber: 2g

    Sugars: 4g

Protein: 4g

DIRECTIONS

1. Mix the rice vinegar, sugar, and salt in a small bowl until the sugar and salt dissolve. Add this mixture to the cooked sushi rice and stir gently to combine. Let it cool slightly.

2. Lay a seaweed sheet on a clean surface, shiny side down. Spread half of the sushi rice evenly over the seaweed sheet, leaving about 1 inch of space at the top.

3. Arrange the tofu strips, avocado slices, cucumber, and carrot in the center of the rice.

4. Carefully roll the seaweed sheet tightly around the filling, using a sushi mat or clean kitchen towel to help if needed. Seal the edge with a bit of water.

5. Repeat with the second seaweed sheet and the remaining ingredients to make the second sushi burrito.

6. Using a sharp knife, slice each sushi burrito in half diagonally.

7. Serve the tofu and avocado sushi burritos with soy sauce, pickled ginger, and wasabi on the side.

Tofu Shawarma Wraps

 4 servings   35 minutes

INGREDIENTS

1 block extra-firm tofu, pressed and sliced into thin strips

4 large whole wheat wraps

1 cup shredded lettuce

1 cup sliced tomatoes

1 cup sliced cucumbers

1/2 cup sliced red onions

1/4 cup chopped fresh parsley

4 tablespoons tahini sauce

2 tablespoons olive oil

2 cloves garlic, minced

1 tablespoon lemon juice

1 teaspoon ground cumin

1 teaspoon paprika

1/2 teaspoon ground coriander

Salt and pepper to taste

DIRECTIONS

1. Preheat your oven to 400°F (200°C).
2. In a small bowl, whisk together olive oil, minced garlic, lemon juice, cumin, paprika, coriander, salt, and pepper.
3. Place the sliced tofu in a shallow dish and pour the marinade. Allow the tofu to marinate for at least 10 minutes.
4. Arrange the marinated tofu strips on a baking sheet lined with parchment paper. Bake in the oven for 20 minutes, flipping halfway through, until the tofu is golden brown and crispy.
5. Warm the whole wheat wraps while the tofu is baking according to package instructions.
6. To assemble the wraps, spread a tablespoon of tahini sauce onto each. Top with shredded lettuce, sliced tomatoes, cucumbers, red onions, and baked tofu strips.
7. Sprinkle chopped parsley over the fillings.
8. Fold the sides of the wrap over the fillings and roll tightly.
9. Serve the tofu shawarma wraps immediately, or wrap them tightly in foil for a portable meal.

NUTRITION INFO

Calories: 320 kcal

Protein: 18g

Fat: 12g

Carbohydrates: 35g

Fiber: 7g

CHAPTER 9

SIDE DISHES

Tofu Fried Rice

 4 servings   30 minutes

INGREDIENTS

2 cups cooked rice
(preferably chilled)
200g firm tofu, pressed
and cubed
2 tablespoons vegetable oil
2 cloves garlic, minced
1 small onion, diced
1 carrot, diced
1/2 cup frozen peas
2 tablespoons soy sauce
1 tablespoon sesame oil
2 green onions, thinly
sliced
Salt and pepper to taste

DIRECTIONS

1. Heat one tablespoon of vegetable oil in a large skillet or wok over medium-high heat.
2. Add the cubed tofu to the skillet and cook until golden brown on all sides, about 5-7 minutes. Remove tofu from the skillet and set aside.
3. In the same skillet, add the remaining tablespoon of vegetable oil. Add minced garlic and diced onion, and cook until softened about 2-3 minutes.
4. Add diced carrot and frozen peas to the skillet, and cook for another 3-4 minutes or until vegetables are tender.
5. Increase the heat to high, then add the cooked rice to the skillet. Stir-fry the rice with the vegetables for about 2-3 minutes.
6. Add the cooked tofu to the skillet, with soy sauce and sesame oil. Stir well to combine all ingredients evenly.
7. Continue cooking for another 2-3 minutes until the tofu is heated and the rice is evenly coated with the sauce.
8. Season with salt and pepper to taste. Garnish with thinly sliced green onions before serving.

NUTRITION INFO

Calories: 15
Total Fat: 0g
Saturated Fat: 0g
Cholesterol: 0mg
Sodium: 45mg

Total Carbohydrate: 3g
Dietary Fiber: 1g
Sugars: 1g
Protein: 1g

Tofu and Quinoa Stuffed Bell Peppers

★★★★★

 4 servings   🕐 50 minutes

INGREDIENTS

4 large bell peppers (any color)

1 cup quinoa, rinsed and drained

1 block (about 14 oz) extra firm tofu, pressed and crumbled

1 tablespoon olive oil

1 small onion, diced

2 cloves garlic, minced

1 teaspoon ground cumin

1 teaspoon smoked paprika

1/2 teaspoon chili powder

Salt and pepper to taste

1 cup canned black beans, drained and rinsed

1 cup corn kernels (fresh, frozen, or canned)

1/2 cup diced tomatoes

1/4 cup chopped fresh cilantro

1/4 cup shredded vegan cheese (optional)

NUTRITION INFO

Calories: 15

Total Fat: 0g

Sodium: 50mg

Total Carbohydrates: 4g

Sugars: 4g

DIRECTIONS

1. Preheat the oven to 375°F (190°C).
2. Cut the tops off the bell peppers and remove the seeds and membranes. Place the peppers in a baking dish, cut side up, and set aside.
3. In a medium saucepan, bring 2 cups of water to a boil. Add the quinoa, reduce the heat to low, cover, and simmer for about 15 minutes, until the quinoa is cooked and the water is absorbed. Remove from heat and fluff with a fork.
4. In a large skillet, heat the olive oil over medium heat. Add the diced onion and cook until softened about 5 minutes. Add the minced garlic, ground cumin, smoked paprika, chilli powder, salt, and pepper. Cook for another 2 minutes, stirring frequently.
5. Add the crumbled tofu to the skillet and cook for 5-7 minutes, until lightly browned.
6. Stir in the cooked quinoa, black beans, corn kernels, diced tomatoes, and chopped cilantro. Cook for an additional 2-3 minutes until heated through.
7. Stuff each bell pepper with the tofu-quinoa mixture, pressing down gently to pack the filling.
8. If using vegan cheese, sprinkle it over the top of each stuffed pepper.
9. Cover the baking dish with aluminium foil and bake in the oven for 20-25 minutes or until the peppers are tender.
10. Remove from the oven and let cool for a few minutes before serving.
11. Serve the stuffed bell peppers with lime wedges on the side.

Tofu and Kale Caesar Salad

 4 servings 15 minutes

INGREDIENTS

1 block (14 oz) extra-firm tofu, drained and pressed

1 bunch kale, stems removed and leaves torn into bite-sized pieces

1 cup cherry tomatoes, halved

1/4 cup grated vegan Parmesan cheese

1/4 cup Caesar dressing (store-bought or homemade)

1 tablespoon olive oil

Salt and pepper to taste

DIRECTIONS

1. Preheat the oven to 400°F (200°C). Cut the pressed tofu into cubes and toss them with olive oil, salt, and pepper on a baking sheet. Bake for 25-30 minutes or until golden brown and crispy.

2. While the tofu is baking, prepare the kale by washing it thoroughly and removing the tough stems. Tear the leaves into bite-sized pieces and place them in a large mixing bowl.

3. Add the halved cherry tomatoes and grated vegan Parmesan cheese to the bowl with the kale.

4. Once the tofu is ready, allow it to cool slightly before adding it to the bowl with the kale and tomatoes.

5. Drizzle the Caesar dressing over the salad and toss everything together until well-coated.

6. Serve the salad immediately, topped with additional vegan Parmesan cheese and croutons if desired.

NUTRITION INFO

Calories: 10

Total Fat: 0g

Saturated Fat: 0g

Cholesterol: 0mg

Sodium: 90mg

Total Carbohydrates: 2g

Dietary Fiber: 1g

Sugars: 1g

Protein: 1g

Tofu and Mushroom Risotto

 4 servings 30 minutes

INGREDIENTS

1 cup Arborio rice

4 cups vegetable broth

1 tablespoon olive oil

1 onion, finely chopped

2 cloves garlic, minced

8 ounces mushrooms, sliced (such as cremini or button)

1 block (14 ounces) firm tofu, drained and cubed

1/2 cup dry white wine (optional)

1/4 cup nutritional yeast (optional)

Salt and pepper to taste

Fresh parsley, chopped (for garnish)

NUTRITION INFO

Calories: 120

Total Fat: 14g

Saturated Fat: 2g

Cholesterol: 0mg

Sodium: 105mg

Total Carbohydrates: 1g

Dietary Fiber: 0g

Sugars: 1g

Protein: 0g

DIRECTIONS

1. Heat the vegetable broth in a medium saucepan over medium heat. Keep it warm while you prepare the risotto.
2. Heat the olive oil over medium heat in a large skillet or saucepan. Add the chopped onion and cook until translucent, about 3-4 minutes.
3. Add the minced garlic and sliced mushrooms to the skillet. Cook until the mushrooms are tender and browned, about 5-6 minutes.
4. Push the mushrooms and onions to one side of the skillet and add the cubed tofu to the empty side. Cook until the tofu is lightly browned on all sides, about 5 minutes.
5. Add the Arborio rice to the skillet and stir to coat it with the oil and juices from the mushrooms and tofu. Cook for 1-2 minutes until the rice is lightly toasted.
6. If using, pour in the white wine and cook until it has evaporated, stirring frequently.
7. Add the warm vegetable broth to the skillet, one ladleful at a time, stirring constantly and allowing the rice to absorb the broth before adding more. Continue this process until the rice is cooked and creamy, about 20-25 minutes. You may only need some of the broth.
8. Once the risotto is creamy and the rice is cooked to your liking, stir in the nutritional yeast (if using) and season with salt and pepper to taste.
9. Serve the tofu and mushroom risotto hot, garnished with chopped fresh parsley.

Tofu Coleslaw with Creamy Dressing

 4 serving　　 15 minutes

INGREDIENTS

1 block (14 oz) firm tofu, drained and pressed

4 cups shredded cabbage (green or purple, or a mix)

1 large carrot, shredded

1/4 cup chopped fresh parsley or cilantro (optional)

Salt and pepper to taste

For the creamy dressing:

1/2 cup vegan mayonnaise

2 tablespoons apple cider vinegar

1 tablespoon maple syrup or agave nectar

1 teaspoon Dijon mustard

1/2 teaspoon garlic powder

DIRECTIONS

1. Begin by preparing the tofu. Cut the pressed tofu into small cubes or strips.
2. In a large mixing bowl, combine the shredded cabbage, carrot, chopped parsley or cilantro (if using), and tofu cubes/strips. Toss gently to mix.
3. In a separate small bowl, whisk together the vegan mayonnaise, apple cider vinegar, maple syrup or agave nectar, Dijon mustard, garlic powder, salt, and pepper until smooth and creamy.
4. Pour the creamy dressing over the coleslaw mixture. Toss until the coleslaw is evenly coated with the dressing.
5. Taste and adjust seasoning if needed with more salt and pepper.
6. Serve immediately as a side dish or refrigerate for 30 minutes to allow the flavours to meld before serving.

NUTRITION INFO

Calories: 45

Total Fat: 0g

Total Carbohydrates: 11g

Sugars: 9g

Protein: 0g

CHAPTER 10

✦ Smoothies and Drinks ✦

Tofu Berry Smoothie

 2 servings 6 minutes

INGREDIENTS

1 cup silken tofu, drained

1 cup mixed berries (such as strawberries, blueberries, raspberries)

1 ripe banana

1/2 cup unsweetened almond milk (or any milk of your choice)

1 tablespoon honey or maple syrup (optional, adjust to taste)

Ice cubes (optional)

DIRECTIONS

1. Combine the silken tofu, mixed berries, ripe banana, and unsweetened almond milk in a blender.
2. Blend on high speed until smooth and creamy. If the smoothie is too thick, add more almond milk, a little at a time, until the desired consistency is reached.
3. Taste the smoothie and add honey or maple syrup if desired for additional sweetness. Blend again until well combined.
4. If you prefer a colder smoothie, add a handful of ice cubes and blend until smooth.
5. Pour the smoothie into glasses and serve immediately. Enjoy your refreshing and nutritious Tofu Berry Smoothie!

NUTRITION INFO

Calories: 15

Total Fat: 0g

Saturated Fat: 0g

Cholesterol: 0mg

Sodium: 45mg

Total Carbohydrate: 3g

Dietary Fiber: 1g

Sugars: 1g

Protein: 1g

Tofu Chocolate Shake

 2 servings   5 minutes

INGREDIENTS

1 block (about 14 ounces) silken tofu, drained

2 tablespoons cocoa powder

2 tablespoons maple syrup or agave nectar

1 teaspoon vanilla extract

1 cup unsweetened almond milk (or any plant-based milk of choice)

1 cup ice cubes

DIRECTIONS

1. Combine the silken tofu, cocoa powder, maple syrup (or agave nectar), vanilla extract, and almond milk in a blender.
2. Blend on high speed until smooth and creamy.
3. Add the ice cubes and blend until the shake is thick and frothy.
4. Taste and adjust sweetness if needed by adding more maple syrup or agave nectar.
5. Pour the chocolate shake into glasses and serve immediately.

NUTRITION INFO

Calories: 15

Total Fat: 0g

Sodium: 50mg

Total Carbohydrates: 4g

Sugars: 4g

Tofu Green Smoothie

 2 servings   10 minutes

INGREDIENTS

1 cup silken tofu

2 cups fresh spinach leaves

1 ripe banana

1 cup pineapple chunks (fresh or frozen)

1 tablespoon honey or maple syrup (optional)

1 cup almond milk (or any milk of your choice)

1 tablespoon chia seeds (optional, for added nutrition)

DIRECTIONS

1. In a blender, combine silken tofu, fresh spinach leaves, ripe banana, pineapple chunks, honey or maple syrup (if using), almond milk, and chia seeds (if using).
2. Blend until smooth and creamy, scraping down the sides of the blender if needed.
3. Please paste the smoothie and adjust sweetness if necessary by adding more honey or maple syrup.
4. Pour the smoothie into glasses and serve immediately, or refrigerate until ready.

NUTRITION INFO

Calories: 215 kcal

Protein: 11g

Fat: 6g

Carbohydrates: 32g

Fiber: 6g

Sugar: 18g

Vitamin A: 122% DV

Vitamin C: 72% DV

Calcium: 27% DV

Iron: 13% DV

Tofu Mango Lassi

★★★★★

2 servings   10 minutes

INGREDIENTS

1 cup ripe mango, chopped

1/2 cup silken tofu

1/2 cup plain yogurt (or dairy-free yogurt for a vegan option)

1/2 cup cold water

2 tablespoons honey or maple syrup (adjust to taste)

1/2 teaspoon ground cardamom

Ice cubes (optional)

Fresh mint leaves for garnish (optional)

DIRECTIONS

1. Combine chopped mango, silken tofu, plain yoghurt, cold water, honey or maple syrup, and ground cardamom in a blender.
2. Blend on high speed until smooth and creamy.
3. Taste and adjust sweetness if needed by adding more honey or maple syrup.
4. If you'd like, please add ice cubes to the blender and blend until smooth and frothy.
5. Pour the Tofu Mango Lassi into glasses.
6. Garnish with fresh mint leaves if desired.
7. Serve immediately and enjoy the refreshing taste of this tropical delight!

NUTRITION INFO

Calories: 180 kcal

Total Fat: 5g

Saturated Fat: 0.5g

Cholesterol: 0mg

Sodium: 20mg

Total Carbohydrates: 28g

Dietary Fiber: 3g

Sugars: 23g

Protein: 9g

Tofu Coffee Frappuccino

 2 serving 10 minutes

INGREDIENTS

1 cup brewed coffee, cooled

1/2 cup silken tofu

1/2 cup almond milk (or any milk of your choice)

2 tablespoons maple syrup (or sweetener of your choice)

1 teaspoon vanilla extract

1 cup ice cubes

Whipped cream (optional, for topping)

Cocoa powder or cinnamon (optional, for garnish)

DIRECTIONS

1. Brew your favourite coffee and cool it to room temperature, or chill it in the refrigerator.
2. Combine the cooled coffee, silken tofu, almond milk, maple syrup, and vanilla extract in a blender.
3. Add the ice cubes to the blender.
4. Blend on high speed until the mixture is smooth and creamy.
5. Taste and adjust sweetness if necessary by adding more maple syrup.
6. Pour the frappuccino into glasses.
7. Top with whipped cream and sprinkle with cocoa powder or cinnamon for garnish.
8. Serve immediately and enjoy your refreshing Tofu Coffee Frappuccino!

NUTRITION INFO

Calories: 90 kcal

Protein: 4g

Fat: 3g

Carbohydrates: 12g

Fiber: 1g

Sugar: 8g

Sodium: 50mg

TOFU

CHAPTER 11

✦ INTERNATIONAL FLAVORS ✦

Tofu Bibimbap (Korean)

 4 servings   60 minutes

INGREDIENTS

1 block firm tofu, drained and pressed

4 cups cooked rice (preferably short-grain or sushi rice)

2 cups mixed vegetables (such as carrots, spinach, mushrooms, and bean sprouts)

4 eggs

4 tablespoons soy sauce

2 tablespoons sesame oil

2 tablespoons gochujang (Korean chili paste)

2 teaspoons sugar

2 cloves garlic, minced

Salt and pepper, to taste

Sesame seeds, for garnish

Vegetable oil, for cooking

DIRECTIONS

1. Slice the pressed tofu into cubes or strips. In a bowl, mix 2 tablespoons of soy sauce, 1 tablespoon of sesame oil, and a pinch of pepper. Add the tofu and marinate for 15-20 minutes.

2. Heat a pan over medium heat and add the marinated tofu. Cook until golden brown on all sides, then set aside.

3. Add more oil if needed in the same pan and sauté the mixed vegetables until tender—season with salt and pepper. Set aside.

4. Mix the remaining soy sauce, sesame oil, gochujang, sugar, and minced garlic in a small bowl to make the bibimbap sauce.

5. In another pan, fry the eggs sunny-side-up or to your liking.

6. To assemble, divide the cooked rice among four bowls. Arrange the cooked tofu and vegetables on top of the rice. Place a fried egg on each bowl.

7. Drizzle the bibimbap sauce over each bowl and sprinkle with sesame seeds.

8. Serve hot and mix everything together before eating.

NUTRITION INFO

Calories: 450

Protein: 20g

Carbohydrates: 60g

Fat: 15g

Fiber: 6g

Sugar: 6g

Sodium: 900mg

Tofu Katsu Curry (Japanese)

4 servings   60 minutes

INGREDIENTS

1 block (14 oz) firm tofu, drained and pressed

1 cup panko breadcrumbs

2 tablespoons all-purpose flour

1 teaspoon garlic powder

1 teaspoon onion powder

Salt and pepper to taste

2 tablespoons vegetable oil

2 cups cooked Japanese short-grain rice, to serve

For the curry sauce:

2 tablespoons vegetable oil

1 onion, finely chopped

2 carrots, peeled and diced

2 potatoes, peeled and diced

2 cloves garlic, minced

2 tablespoons curry powder

3 cups vegetable broth

2 tablespoons soy sauce

1 tablespoon honey or sugar

DIRECTIONS

1. Prepare the tofu: Cut the tofu into four equal-sized pieces. Season with salt and pepper. Dredge each piece in flour, dip in beaten egg, and coat with panko breadcrumbs.

2. Fry the tofu: Heat vegetable oil in a large pan over medium heat. Fry the tofu until golden brown and crispy, about 4-5 minutes per side. Transfer to a paper towel-lined plate to drain excess oil.

3. Make the curry sauce: Heat some vegetable oil over medium heat in a separate pan. Add the onion, carrots, and potatoes. Sauté for 5-7 minutes until vegetables start to soften. Add garlic, curry powder, and flour. Cook for another minute.

4. Simmer the curry: Slowly pour the vegetable broth, soy sauce, ketchup, and honey or sugar. Stir well to combine. Bring to a simmer and cook for 15-20 minutes or until the vegetables are tender and the sauce has thickened.

5. Serve: Slice the tofu into strips. Serve the tofu katsu over rice with the curry sauce. Garnish with pickled vegetables if desired. Enjoy!

Tofu Tikka (Indian)

 4 servings 30 minutes

INGREDIENTS

1 block (about 14 oz or 400g) extra-firm tofu, pressed and cubed

1 cup plain yogurt (use dairy-free yogurt for a vegan option)

2 tablespoons tikka masala spice blend

1 tablespoon lemon juice

1 tablespoon vegetable oil

1 teaspoon ground cumin

1 teaspoon ground coriander

1 teaspoon paprika

1 teaspoon garam masala

Salt to taste

Fresh cilantro leaves, chopped, for garnish

DIRECTIONS

1. Mix the yoghurt, tikka masala spice blend, lemon juice, vegetable oil, ground cumin, coriander, paprika, garam masala, and salt in a bowl.
2. Add the cubed tofu to the marinade and gently toss until well coated. Cover the bowl and let it marinate in the refrigerator for at least 1 hour, preferably overnight.
3. Preheat the oven to 400°F (200°C). Line a baking sheet with parchment paper.
4. Arrange the marinated tofu cubes on the prepared baking sheet in a single layer.
5. Bake the tofu in the oven for 20-25 minutes, flipping halfway through or until the tofu is golden brown and slightly crispy on the edges.
6. Once cooked, remove the tofu tikka from the oven and transfer it to a serving platter.
7. Garnish with chopped cilantro leaves and serve hot with lemon wedges on the side.

NUTRITION INFO

Calories: 210 kcal

Protein: 14g

Fat: 12g

Carbohydrates: 11g

Fiber: 2g

Tofu Tacos with Chipotle Lime Crema (Mexican)

 4 servings 40 minutes

INGREDIENTS

1 block (14 oz) extra firm tofu, drained and pressed

2 tablespoons olive oil

1 teaspoon chili powder

1 teaspoon cumin

1/2 teaspoon smoked paprika

Chipotle Lime Crema:

1/2 cup vegan mayonnaise

1 chipotle pepper in adobo sauce, minced

1 tablespoon lime juice

1 teaspoon lime zest

Salt to taste

Taco Assembly:

8 small corn tortillas, warmed

1 cup shredded lettuce

1 cup diced tomatoes

1/2 cup chopped cilantro

DIRECTIONS

1. Preheat the oven to 400°F (200°C).
2. Slice the pressed tofu into thin strips.
3. In a bowl, whisk together the olive oil, soy sauce, chilli powder, cumin, garlic powder, salt, and pepper. Add the tofu strips and toss to coat.
4. Place the tofu strips on a baking sheet lined with parchment paper. Bake for 15-20 minutes, flipping halfway through, until the tofu is crispy and golden brown.
5. While the tofu is baking, prepare the chipotle lime crema. In a small bowl, mix the vegan sour cream, minced chipotle pepper, adobo sauce, lime juice, and salt. Adjust seasoning to taste.
6. Heat the corn tortillas in a skillet over medium heat until warm and pliable.
7. To assemble the tacos, place some shredded lettuce on each tortilla, followed by the baked tofu strips. Top with diced tomatoes, red onion, and cilantro. Drizzle with chipotle lime crema and serve with lime wedges on the side.

NUTRITION INFO

Calories: 325

Fat: 16g

Carbohydrates: 34g

Fiber: 6g

Protein: 13g

Tofu Pad See Ew (Thai)

 4 serving   30 minutes

INGREDIENTS

8 ounces wide rice noodles

2 tablespoons vegetable oil

3 cloves garlic, minced

8 ounces firm tofu, pressed and cut into cubes

2 cups broccoli florets

1 cup sliced carrots

1 cup sliced bell peppers (any color)

3 tablespoons soy sauce

2 tablespoons oyster sauce (or vegetarian oyster sauce)

1 tablespoon brown sugar

1 tablespoon rice vinegar

1 teaspoon sesame oil

NUTRITION INFO

Calories: 90 kcal

Protein: 4g

Fat: 3g

Carbohydrates: 12g

Fiber: 1g

Sugar: 8g

Sodium: 50mg

DIRECTIONS

1. Cook the rice noodles according to package instructions until al dente. Drain and set aside.
2. Whisk together the soy sauce, oyster sauce, brown sugar, rice vinegar, and sesame oil in a small bowl. Set aside.
3. Heat one tablespoon of vegetable oil in a large skillet or wok over medium-high heat. Add the minced garlic and cook for about 30 seconds until fragrant.
4. Add the tofu cubes to the skillet in a single layer. Cook for 3-4 minutes on each side until golden brown. Remove the tofu from the skillet and set aside.
5. Add the remaining tablespoon of vegetable oil to the skillet. Add the broccoli florets, sliced carrots, and bell peppers. Stir-fry for 4-5 minutes until the vegetables are tender-crisp.
6. Return the tofu to the skillet with the vegetables. Add the cooked rice noodles and the prepared sauce. Toss everything together until well combined and heated through about 2-3 minutes.
7. Taste and adjust seasoning if necessary. If you prefer a saucier dish, add a splash of water or vegetable broth.
8. Remove from heat and serve hot, garnished with sliced green onions and crushed peanuts if desired. Enjoy your delicious Tofu Pad. See Ew!

CONCLUSION

As you close this cookbook, envision a culinary journey that transcends the mere act of cooking; it's a voyage of discovery, creativity, and nourishment, both for the body and the soul. In these pages, you've embarked on an adventure through the versatile world of tofu, where humble soybean curd transforms into exquisite culinary delights.

But this journey isn't just about mastering recipes; it's about embracing a new perspective—a shift towards sustainable eating, compassionate cooking, and mindful living. With each dish crafted from this cookbook's heart, you've explored new flavours and textures and contributed to a more vibrant, healthier planet.

As you savour the last bite of your Tofu Pad See Ew or indulge in a velvety Tofu Chocolate Mousse, remember that every ingredient holds a story, and every recipe is possible. Whether you're a novice in the kitchen or a seasoned chef, this cookbook has been your trusted companion, guiding you through the artistry of tofu cuisine with simplicity and grace.

So, as you set down this book, let its essence linger in your kitchen, infusing every meal with creativity and joy. May these recipes inspire your culinary endeavours, sparking moments of connection, celebration, and pure culinary bliss. And as you continue to explore the vast landscape of plant-based cooking, remember that the adventure never truly ends—it only grows richer with each delicious chapter.

Bon appétit, and may your culinary journey be as fulfilling as the flavours you create!

About THE AUTHOR

Hello, culinary adventurers!
I'm Vakare Rimkute, a passionate explorer of the culinary world and a devoted recipe book writer. With a whisk in one hand and a pen in the other, I traverse the realms of flavor, seeking to blend tradition with innovation in every dish I create.

Growing up in the bustling kitchens of my Lithuanian grandmother, I developed an insatiable curiosity for the alchemy of ingredients and the magic they could weave on the palate. From the rustic charm of hearty stews to the delicate intricacies of pastries, my journey through food has been nothing short of a delightful adventure.

After years of experimenting and honing my craft, I found my true calling as a recipe book writer. With each recipe I pen, I aim to capture the essence of culinary culture while infusing it with a touch of modern flair. From comforting classics to bold culinary experiments, my recipes are a reflection of my belief that food should not only nourish the body but also nourish the soul.

So join me on this gastronomic journey, where every page is filled with tantalizing flavors, heartwarming stories, and a dash of humor. Together, let's embark on a culinary adventure that will tickle your taste buds and leave you craving for more. Happy cooking!

Weekly Meal Planner

Week _____   Month _____

Monday

Breakfast _____

Lunch _____

Dinner _____

Snacks _____

Tuesday

Breakfast _____

Lunch _____

Dinner _____

Snacks _____

Wednesday

Breakfast _____

Lunch _____

Dinner _____

Snacks _____

Thursday

Breakfast _____

Lunch _____

Dinner _____

Snacks _____

Friday

Breakfast _____

Lunch _____

Dinner _____

Snacks _____

Saturday

Breakfast _____

Lunch _____

Dinner _____

Snacks _____

Sunday

Breakfast _____

Lunch _____

Dinner _____

Snacks _____

Notes

Weekly Meal Planner

Week _____   Month _____

Monday

Breakfast _____

Lunch _____

Dinner _____

Snacks _____

Tuesday

Breakfast _____

Lunch _____

Dinner _____

Snacks _____

Wednesday

Breakfast _____

Lunch _____

Dinner _____

Snacks _____

Thursday

Breakfast _____

Lunch _____

Dinner _____

Snacks _____

Friday

Breakfast _____

Lunch _____

Dinner _____

Snacks _____

Saturday

Breakfast _____

Lunch _____

Dinner _____

Snacks _____

Sunday

Breakfast _____

Lunch _____

Dinner _____

Snacks _____

Notes

Weekly Meal Planner

Week _____   Month _____

Monday

Breakfast _____

Lunch _____

Dinner _____

Snacks _____

Tuesday

Breakfast _____

Lunch _____

Dinner _____

Snacks _____

Wednesday

Breakfast _____

Lunch _____

Dinner _____

Snacks _____

Thursday

Breakfast _____

Lunch _____

Dinner _____

Snacks _____

Friday

Breakfast _____

Lunch _____

Dinner _____

Snacks _____

Saturday

Breakfast _____

Lunch _____

Dinner _____

Snacks _____

Sunday

Breakfast _____

Lunch _____

Dinner _____

Snacks _____

Notes

Weekly Meal Planner

Week _____   Month _____

Monday

Breakfast _____
Lunch _____
Dinner _____
Snacks _____

Tuesday

Breakfast _____
Lunch _____
Dinner _____
Snacks _____

Wednesday

Breakfast _____
Lunch _____
Dinner _____
Snacks _____

Thursday

Breakfast _____
Lunch _____
Dinner _____
Snacks _____

Friday

Breakfast _____
Lunch _____
Dinner _____
Snacks _____

Saturday

Breakfast _____
Lunch _____
Dinner _____
Snacks _____

Sunday

Breakfast _____
Lunch _____
Dinner _____
Snacks _____

Notes

Weekly Meal Planner

Week _____   Month _____

Monday

Breakfast _____

Lunch _____

Dinner _____

Snacks _____

Tuesday

Breakfast _____

Lunch _____

Dinner _____

Snacks _____

Wednesday

Breakfast _____

Lunch _____

Dinner _____

Snacks _____

Thursday

Breakfast _____

Lunch _____

Dinner _____

Snacks _____

Friday

Breakfast _____

Lunch _____

Dinner _____

Snacks _____

Saturday

Breakfast _____

Lunch _____

Dinner _____

Snacks _____

Sunday

Breakfast _____

Lunch _____

Dinner _____

Snacks _____

Notes

Weekly Meal Planner

Week _____   Month _____

Monday

Breakfast _____

Lunch _____

Dinner _____

Snacks _____

Tuesday

Breakfast _____

Lunch _____

Dinner _____

Snacks _____

Wednesday

Breakfast _____

Lunch _____

Dinner _____

Snacks _____

Thursday

Breakfast _____

Lunch _____

Dinner _____

Snacks _____

Friday

Breakfast _____

Lunch _____

Dinner _____

Snacks _____

Saturday

Breakfast _____

Lunch _____

Dinner _____

Snacks _____

Sunday

Breakfast _____

Lunch _____

Dinner _____

Snacks _____

Notes

Weekly Meal Planner

Week _____   Month _____

Monday

Breakfast _____

Lunch _____

Dinner _____

Snacks _____

Tuesday

Breakfast _____

Lunch _____

Dinner _____

Snacks _____

Wednesday

Breakfast _____

Lunch _____

Dinner _____

Snacks _____

Thursday

Breakfast _____

Lunch _____

Dinner _____

Snacks _____

Friday

Breakfast _____

Lunch _____

Dinner _____

Snacks _____

Saturday

Breakfast _____

Lunch _____

Dinner _____

Snacks _____

Sunday

Breakfast _____

Lunch _____

Dinner _____

Snacks _____

Notes

Made in the USA
Las Vegas, NV
12 November 2024